BLACKBIRDS & BOOKWORMS

Just how slow is a sloth really?

...and 100 other fun facts about animals

EMERALD PENGUIN MEDIA GROUP

COPYRIGHT © 2021 BY EMERALD PENGUIN MEDIA GROUP

All rights reserved. No part of this book may be reproduced in any form on by an electronic or mechanical means, including information storage and retrieval systems, without permission in writing from the publisher, except by a reviewer who may quote brief passages in a review.

ISBN 978-1-008-93208-1
Imprint: Lulu.com

CONTENTS

Bears .... page 1
Koalas .... page 2
Elephants .... page 3
Sharks & dolphins .... page 4
Whales .... page 5
Sea animals .... page 6
Pelicans .... page 8
Puffins .... page 9
On the farm .... page 10
Geese .... page 11
Ducks .... page 12
Chickens .... page 13
Goats .... page 14
Horses .... page 15
Animals you see at night .... page 16
Otters .... page 17
Reindeer .... page 18
Moose .... page 19
Sloths .... page 20
Flamingos & ostriches .... page 21
In the field .... page 22
Bats .... page 23
Monkeys .... page 24
Gorillas .... page 25
Critters .... page 26
Bees .... page 27

Hi!

We're Blackbirds & Bookworms.

We chose the name because blackbirds are curious creatures, and often seen as a symbol of intelligence, and bookworms are, well, bookworms!

We want to make learning easy, interesting, and fun.

Not the kind of things you would learn just anywhere though, no. Our facts are unusual, unique, and sometimes just plain strange - but we know you'll enjoy them anyway!

BEARS

THERE ARE EIGHT SPECIES OF BEAR

The North American black bear, Asiatic black bear, Andean bear, brown bear, polar bear, panda bear, sloth bear, and sun bear.

WAIT... POLAR BEARS DON'T HAVE WHITE FUR?

No, they don't! Their outer fur is mostly hollow and transparent. The hair actually reflects light, which makes the fur look white!

GRIZZLY BEARS EAT HOW MUCH?!

Grizzly bears (a type of brown bear) have to eat lots of food so they can safely hibernate during the winter! They eat up to 41kg of food every day! That's about the same weight 14 standard bricks! Yikes!

KOALAS

KOALA BEARS AREN'T BEARS?

No, they're not! Koalas are marsupials - a group of animals that climb into their mother's pouch after they're born.

THEY LIVE IN THE EUCALYPTUS FORESTS IN AUSTRALIA

And they eat a lot of eucalyptus leaves! Koalas normally eat around 500g to 800g of Eucalyptus leaves every day!

BABY KOALAS ARE CALLED JOEYS

And they're born blind and earless! They use their strong sense of touch and smell to find and climb into their mother's pouch where they grow for about six months. Then, when they're strong enough, they'll ride around on their mother's back for another six months!

ELEPHANTS

THEY ARE THE WORLD'S LARGEST LAND ANIMAL

Males generally measure up to 3 metres high and can weigh up to 6,000kg. Baby elephants can weigh 120kg!

AND THEY SPEND MOST OF THE DAY EATING!

They spend 80% of their day eating! Probably because they have to eat so much - 150kg of food! That's the same weight as 1.5 pandas!

HOW LONG CAN THEY LIVE?

Well, that depends on the species, but many elephants can live up to 70 years old!

BABY ELEPHANTS SUCK THEIR TRUNKS WHEN THEY'RE UPSET?

(just like how baby humans suck their thumbs).

SHARKS & DOLPHINS

THERE ARE **OVER** 400 SPECIES OF SHARK IN THE WORLD...

AND THEIR SKIN IS COVERED IN MINIATURE TEETH CALLED 'DERMAL DENTICLES'

ONLY ONE HALF OF A DOLPHIN'S BRAIN SLEEPS AT A TIME!

The other half remains away to make the dolphin come up for air when needed.

AND BOTTLENOSE DOLPHINS ARE ONE OF THE FEW SPECIES THAT RECOGNISE THEMSELVES IN A MIRROR!

WHALES

THERE ARE TWO GROUPS OF WHALE

Baleen whales and toothed whales. Baleen whales have fibrous plates in their mouths instead of teeth and toothed whales have... well, teeth.

A HUMPBACK WHALE'S FLIPPERS CAN GROW UP TO 5 METRES LONG!

Which means they are the animal with the largest appendage (external body part) in the world!

NARWHALS ARE WHALES WITH A SPIRALLED TOOTH!

That may look like a horn but it's actually a long tooth called a 'tusk'. They sometimes use their tusks to joust other narwhals.

SEA ANIMALS

OCTOPUSES HAVE THREE HEARTS!
And they can taste and grab with the suckers on their arms!

GIANT ARCTIC JELLYFISH HAVE TENTACLES THAT CAN REACH OVER 36 METRES IN LENGTH!

SEAHORSES MATE FOR LIFE AND HOLD EACH OTHER'S TAIL WHEN THEY TRAVEL

STARFISH DO NOT HAVE A BRAIN OR ANY BLOOD!

Instead of blood, seawater is pumped throughout their body.

TURTLES CAN BREATHE THROUGH THEIR BUTTS?!

Yes, indeed! Some types of turtles breathe through their butts because it's easier to do that than breathe through their mouths, due the structure of their shell!

STINGRAYS ARE CLOSELY RELATED TO SHARKS

They also have no bones in their body! Their entire skeleton is made up of cartilage (the bendy stuff at the tip of your nose)!

CORAL IS ACTUALLY AN ANIMAL, NOT A PLANT!

PELICANS

THE PELICAN FAMILY IS AT LEAST 30 MILLION YEARS OLD

SOME PELICANS FISH BY SWIMMING IN GROUPS

They form a line or a "U" shape and beat their wings on the surface to drive fish into shallow water so they can scoop them up.

BUT BROWN PELICANS DIVE FOR FISH FROM ABOVE AND SNARE THEM IN THEIR BILL!

THE AMERICAN WHITE PELICAN CAN HOLD ABOUT 3 GALLONS OF WATER IN ITS BILL

PUFFINS

THERE ARE FOUR SPECIES OF PUFFIN
The Atlantic puffin, Horned puffin, Tufted puffin and Rhinoceros Auklet.

THEIR BEAK (OR BILL) CHANGES COLOUR DURING THE YEAR
They only have a colourful beak during the Spring breeding season. Just before winter, they shed their colourful outer beak, which leaves behind a smaller and duller-coloured beak.

THEY MATE FOR LIFE
They generally pair up with the same partner as previous years to raise their puffling (baby puffin) over the summer and then return the following year with the same mate to the same burrow (a hole they dig in the earth and sides of cliffs with their beaks and feet) to raise their puffling.

ON THE FARM

COWS ONLY HAVE ONE STOMACH...

...but it has four separate chambers to allow the animal to break down plant matter that normally wouldn't be digestable.

SHEEP HAVE RECTANGULAR PUPILS!

This means they can see almost 360 degrees and look behind themselves without turning their heads! Freaky!

PIGS ARE ACTUALLY VERY CLEAN ANIMALS

Their reputation as a dirty animal is because they roll in mud to cool down because they cannot sweat. Pigs that live in cool environments stay clean!

GEESE

'GOOSE' IS ACTUALLY THE TERM FOR FEMALE GEESE

Male geese are called ganders.

A GROUP OF GEESE IS CALLED A GAGGLE...

...but only when they are on land or in water. When a group of geese are in the air they are called a skein.

MANY BRREDS OF GEESE MIGRATE FOR THE WINTER

They fly up to 5,000 kilometres each season. They fly as a gaggle and will fly in a V-shaped formation so they can stay close together during their long journey.

DUCKS

THEIR FEATHERS ARE VERY WATERPROOF!
This is because their feathers interlock and are covered in a waxy coating. So even when they dive underwater, their skin stays completely dry.

THEY CANNOT GET COLD FEET...
...because they have no nerves or blood vessels in their feet! So don't worry if you ever see a duck standing in the snow!

THEY LAY MORE EGGS IF IT'S SUNNY

BABY DUCKS (DUCKLINGS) CAN WALK AND SWIM HOURS AFTER HATCHING!
But they can't fly until they are two months old because they aren't born with flight feathers.

CHICKENS

THEY HAVE GREAT MEMORIES
They can remember more than 100 faces - both human and animal!

THEY CAN ALSO RUN AS FAST AS 9 MILES AN HOUR!
But only for short bursts

FEMALE BABY CHICKENS ARE CALLED PULLETS AND BABY MALES ARE CALLED COCKERELS

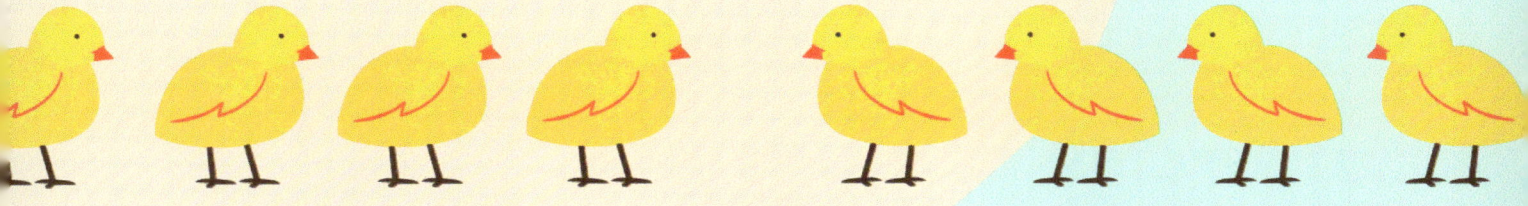

THE FATHER (ROOSTER) PROTECTS THE HENS AND CHICKS BY WATCHING FOR DANGER TO KEEP PREDATORS AWAY

GOATS

A GOAT GIVING BIRTH IS CALLED A KIDDING...

...because a baby goat is called a kid!

KIDS MAKE UNIQUE SOUNDS

And mother goats use these sounds and a kid's scent to recognise them.

YOU MAY HAVE HEARD THAT THEY EAT EVERYTHING IN SIGHT...

...but they are actually very picky eaters! They have very sensitive lips and will often refuse to eat hay that is dirty or old.

AND THEY ARE VERY GOOD AT CLIMBING

They often live on mountains and have even been known to climb to the top of trees!

HORSES

THEY TAKE SHORT NAPS DURING THE DAY

They need about 3 hours sleep every day but they do this by taking several short naps (about 10-30 minutes) throughout the day.

AND THEY MAINLY NAP STANDING UP

Because they are big animals so laying down for long periods of time can be dangerous. They only lie down to dream.

YOU CAN ESTIMATE THEIR AGE BY LOOKING AT THEIR TEETH!

AND MEASURE THEIR HEIGHT IN 'HANDS'

One 'hand' is the same as 4 inches

ANIMALS AT NIGHT-TIME

HEDGEHOGS HAVE OVER 5000 SPIKES (QUILLS)
Each spine/quill falls out and is replaced every year

A FEMALE FOX IS CALLED A VIXEN
And they can give birth to between one and eleven pups! Vixens live in underground dens with their litter of pups for seven months whilst they grow.

RACCOONS RINSE THEIR FOOD BEFORE EATING IT
If there is no water nearby, they will rub their food to remove any dirt.

OTTERS

THEY OFTEN KEEP A ROCK IN THE SKIN UNDER THEIR ARMS

They use these rocks to break open shelled animals (like clams.

SEA OTTERS OFTEN HOLD HANDS WHEN THEY SLEEP

So that they don't drift away from each other (and their food).

AND MOTHERS CARRY AND NURSE THEIR PUPS ON THEIR BELLIES WHEN FLOATING ON THEIR BACK

THEY ALSO WRAP THEIR PUPS IN STRANDS OF KELP

(to stop them floating out to the ocean)

REINDEER

THEY LIVE IN VERY COLD PLACES
Like the Arctic tundra, Greenland, Scandinavia, Russia, Alaska, and Canada, so they have adapted to the cold.

THEY ARE THE ONLY SPECIES OF DEER WHERE BOTH THE MALE AND FEMALE CAN GROW ANTLERS!

THEIR HOOVES SHRINK IN THE WINTER...
...when the ground is harder and then they expand in the summer when the ground is softer!

THEIR EYEBALLS DO WHAT?!
They turn blue in the winter to help them see in low-light. We guess 'Rudolph the Blue Eyed Reindeer' wasn't as catchy?

MOOSE

THEY ARE THE LARGEST OF ALL THE DEER SPECIES!

They can weigh up to 544kg and can grow to 2 metres tall (not including antlers)!

ONLY MALE MOOSE (BULLS) HAVE ANTLERS

AND THEY SHED THEM EVERY WINTER

(but they grow back in the Spring)

THEY ARE EXCELLENT SWIMMERS

They can dive more than 5 metres underwater for food, and can hold their breath for a minute. Even calves can go for long swims a few days after birth!

FEMALES (COWS) OFTEN GIVE BIRTH TO TWINS - AND SOMETIMES TRIPLETS!

SLOTHS

CAN SPEND 90% OF THEIR LIVES HANGING UPSIDE DOWN!

This is because their organs are attached to their ribcage, so they can hang upside down without it effecting their breathing!

THEY POOP WHAT?

Sloths don't poop very often (roughly they poop once a week) so when they do go they end up pooping a third of their body weight in one go!

SO, JUST HOW SLOW IS A SLOTH REALLY?

Well, they are the slowest mammal alive! They rarely leave the treetops but when they do, they only crawl 30 cm a minute!

BUT THEY SWIM THREE TIMES FASTER THAN THEY CRAWL!

FLAMINGOS & OSTRICHES

FLAMINGOS HAVE PINK FEATHERS BECAUSE OF THEIR DIET!

They eat certain algae which contains a pigment called carotenoid (the same pigment that makes carrots orange). Flamingos also eat shrimp and other shrimp-like creatures that are pink because they too also eat the algae that turns them pink!

BABY FLAMINGOS HATCH IN A NEST MADE OF MUD

OSTRICHES ARE VERY BIG!

They can grow up to 2.7 metres tall and weigh as much as 159 kg!

BUT THEY ARE SUPER SPEEDY!

They can reach speeds of over 70 kilometres per hour!

IN THE FIELD

MICE EAT BETWEEN 15 AND 20 TIMES A DAY...

...but they produce between 40 and 100 droppings (poop) per day!

CROWS HOLD GRUDGES

Scientists have seen that crows remember people who have been mean to them, and ignore them or even attack them if they see them again!

RABBITS PURR WHEN RELAXED...

AND THEY CAN TURN THEIR EARS 270 DEGREES...

...independently of each other, so they can pay attention to different sounds and listen out for any predators! Plus, their long ears can grow up to 10 centimetres in length, so they are definitely great listeners!

BATS

THEY CAN EAT UP TO 1,200 MOSQUITOES AN HOUR!

And very often eat their body weight in insects every night.

BABY BATS ARE CALLED PUPS!

THEY'RE BORN UPSIDE-DOWN!

Yes, you read that correctly! Bats are born upside-down so their mum's have to catch them before they fall!

AND THEY CAN WEIGH UP TO A THIRD OF THEIR MUM'S BODY WEIGHT!

MANY BATS FIND THEIR FOOD IN THE DARK

Many bats are nocturnal (which means they're awake at night-time) so they cannot see their food. Insted they make high-pitched sounds and listen to the echoes. This is called echolocation.

MONKEYS

THERE ARE AROUND 260 SPECIES OF MONKEY

Most of them live in trees but a few species prefer the ground (like baboons)!

THEY HAVE LONG ARMS AND LONG LEGS TO HELP THEM SWING FROM TREES

AND SOME MONKEYS USE THEIR TAILS TO GRASP OBJECTS!

These tails are called 'prehensile', which means 'able to grasp'. Some monkeys also use their tails to dangle from branches!

THEY PICK BUGS AND DIRT OFF OTHER MONKEYS IF THEY LIKE THEM!

GORILLAS

WE SHARE AROUND 98% OF OUR DNA WITH GORILLAS

THEY ARE VERY INTELLIGENT
They can use some tools and even learn sign language!

AND ARE GENERALLY HERBIVORES (EAT VEGETABLES)...
...but they are known to eat small animals and insects occassionally.

THEIR ARMS ARE LONGER THAN THEIR LEGS
So they walk on all four limbs and still stay slightly upright.

CRITTERS

THERE ARE BETWEEN SIX AND TEN MILLION DIFFERENT TYPES OF INSECTS!

They come in all shapes, colours, and sizes but they all have six legs, three parts to their body, and two antennae on their heads!

THE NUMBER OF SPOTS ON A LADYBIRD WILL TELL YOU WHAT SPECIES IT BELONGS TO

Not the age of the ladybird as you may have thought! And considering there are over 6,000 species of ladybird, knowing how to tell them apart is important!

SOME CATTERPILLARS EAT 27,000 TIMES THEIR OWN BODY WEIGHT IN THE FIRST FEW WEEKS OF THEIR LIFE!

They have to do this because the food they eat as a catterpillar has to last them when they transform into a butterfly!

BEES

BEES HAVE FOUR WINGS, NOT TWO!

The wings hook hook together to form a big pair of wings whilst flying!

SOME SPECIES LIKE TO STAY BY THEMSELVES

These are called 'solitary bees' and they do not live in hives or make honey. Instead, females work alone to collect materials so they can build nests inside hollow stalks or holes in soil, sand, clay, and wood.

BUT MOST SPECIES LIVE IN HIVES OR COLONIES

And there are three types of bees that live in the hive/colony - drones, workers, and a queen.

A SINGLE WORKER HONEYBEE MAKES ONE TWELFTH OF A TEASPOON OF HONEY IN THEIR LIFETIME!

However, the entire colony produces 100 kg of honey every year!

COMING SOON

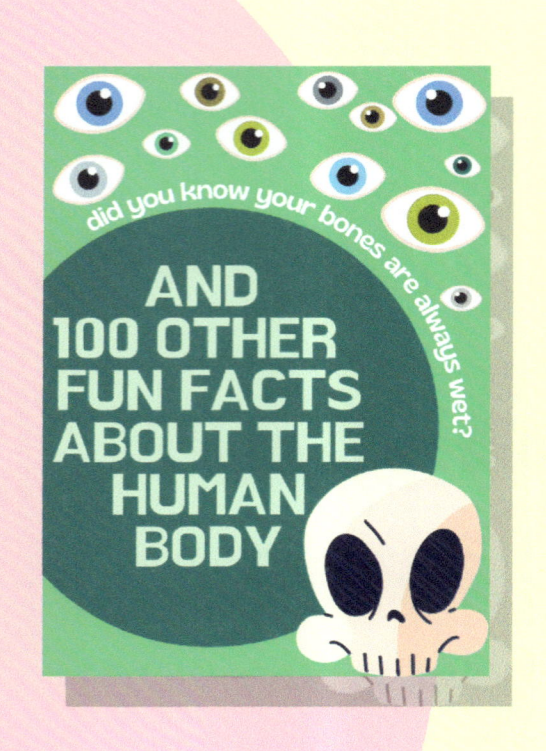

DID YOU KNOW YOUR BONES ARE ALWAYS WET? AND 100 OTHER FUN FACTS ABOUT THE HUMAN BODY

BANANAS GROW ON TREES! AND 100 OTHER THINGS YOU PROBABLY THOUGHT WERE TRUE

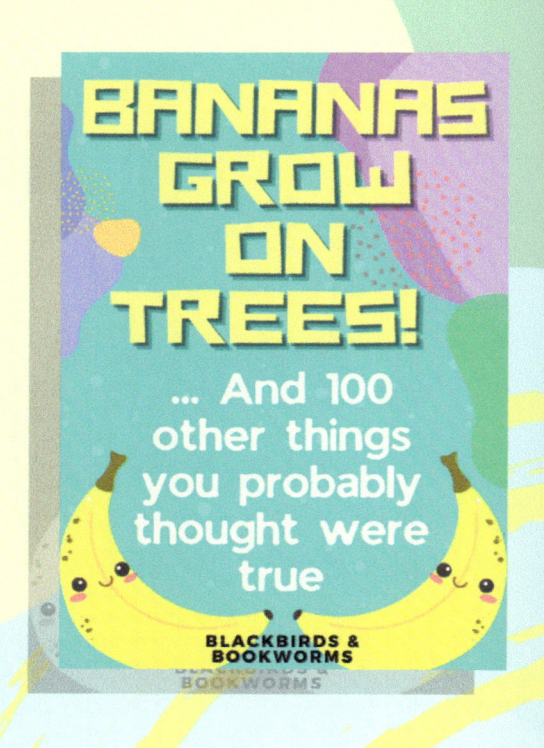